Dream Symbols Made Easy

(Simple Steps to Analyzing and Understanding Dreams)

Jeanie P. Johnson

A comprehensive and easily learned method in remembering what dream symbols mean and putting them into practice.

Copyright 2016

Jeanie P. Johnson

Jeanie P. Johnson

THE DREAMING SELF

Since the dawn of time man has been intrigued with dreams. In the Bible there were many instances where dreams came into play and were interpreted by those who were considered seers or prophets. There have been metaphorical people who add their hand at interpreting dreams.   Many books and dictionaries have been published to explain meanings of dreams.   Scientists and dream therapist have studied dreams and how we dream, and though they have all come up with very interesting findings about dreams and dreaming, no one seems to have come up with an easy way to interpret your own dreams, without having to carry around a dream dictionary in your hip pocket.

The reasons, I feel that dreams are so hard to understand, is that we really do not understand what dreams are all about and even why we dream. There are all sorts of theories and attitudes about it, but in all the theories no one has put down any real helpful steps that I believed anyone who knows nothing about analyzing dreams can follow easily, in order to know what their dreams mean.

In this book, I plan to put down my theories concerning dreams, gained through many sources. This is a compilation of information I have read, and agreed with, along with my own methods, which I have put to use in my own life. It also takes in my own dreams and how I have managed to interpret them, and the process I have used to do it with. It is also from information that I have received through channeling, and from my views through studying how reality works and how dreams are connected with our reality.

I think the main reason people do not understand dreams, is they do not know how their reality is created and the part that dreams play in creating your reality. Also, because there are many different types of dreams, people don't realize that you can't just lump all dreams up into one category, and then start giving meanings to them. It is up to the dreamer to know and recognize just what kind of dream they are dreaming, before they will ever be able to discover what the dream means.

Also, as helpful as dream dictionaries are, you can't just assume that what one person dreams about will have the same meaning if another person dreams about the same thing. Because of our own unique relationship with how we respond to our realities, each dream has to be geared around our own belief system and how we perceive life. One thing that may be frightening to one person may not frighten another. Therefore, only the dreamer can decide if they are having a nightmare or not, even if two people are both dreaming the same dream. Something that may be pleasant to one person, may not be pleasant to another. It may appear to be a good omen to the one that dreams that the experience is pleasant, where someone else may consider it a bad omen, though the experience seems identical in the dream. So if only the beholder can know the actual meaning of the dream, how can a book tell you what your dream means?

In this book, I am not going to try and tell you what your dream means. What I am going to do is to explain to you how dreams are crated, why they are created, the difference between one type of dream and another, and the symbolism of dreams. Once you know the symbolism of dreams, analyzing dreams will become very simple.

The simplicity of symbolism is that once you start to learn it, even if I don't give you the symbols for everything you dream about, you will understand how to guess the symbols yourself. In addition, where a dictionary may have pages upon pages of interpretations that you could never memorize, one symbol may cover many areas of your dream, which make it easier to remember major symbols and then use common sense to elaborate on those major symbol when you see them in your dreams.

Since dreaming relates to life itself, we must first understand life and how it works. Since my philosophy incorporates reincarnation, it will be more difficult for those who do not believe it reincarnation to grasp the whole concept of dreaming, so to include those who do not believe in past lives, but do believe in life after death, consider this. Even if you have never lived in the physical prior to this life, you must believe that you did exist in some form before coming to the earth. Therefore, your past life would be that life you lived with God before you came to this earth. Your present life would be the experience that you are having now, and your future lives, or life is the one that will take place after you die and go to heaven or hell or purgatory, for that matter.

Even Christians believe that what they did before they came to this earth in some way effects what is happening to them right now. If they were a good and faithful servant before coming here they strive to be one now. If they fell short, then maybe all their trials and tribulations here were caused by that lack of faith and they must work through it now. They also believe if they perform correctly, keeping God's commandments here on earth and taking upon them the name of Jesus Christ, that their reward will be to dwell with God once more.

Some of what dreams do is to let you know how well you are performing in the here and now, and how it is effecting and will affect your life. They also show you how you are responding to your lessons here, or trials. They may give you glimpses into the future so you are prepared for new lessons. If you believe in reincarnation, they show you what you learned in past lives and how it is effecting this life, and how it could affect future lives if your attitude stays the same as it is at the time you have the dream. If you don't believe in reincarnation, then you can consider that dreams dealing with past experiences can be experiences when you were younger, during this life. They could also be experiences from your pre-existence showing how they are effecting your physical existence, which could affect your chances of a future existence with God. However, taking in the concept of reincarnation makes dreams a lot simpler to understand and respond to. Therefore, I am going to take the approach to dreams from a reincarnation standpoint.

Life and Dreaming

Before we come to this earthly existence, we are well aware of our purpose for being here and what sort of lessons we are supposed to learn. Our inner self is the consciousness that is aware of this information. When we come to this earth, we no longer remember the things the inner is aware of and we are only aware of experience and physical knowledge. This is our outer consciousness. When we dream, our inner consciousness, or subconscious, is the one that is active, because it is correlating all of our experiences in this existence and others, whether they be pre-existence or past lives. It knows what we wish to achieve in our future existence, whether they be our future life here on this earth, future lives we may live again, or our life after we die and leave this world. It knows all the ways we can accomplish all our goals whether, physical or spiritual. It knows all the ways we have attempted to accomplish them. It knows what has worked, what won't work and what will work. If we are using any of those methods, it knows at what point in our lives they have or will affect us. It knows how we are progressing and how we will continue to progress if we continue on the same path we were on at the time of the dream.

It's job is to communicate with our outer consciousness and make it aware of some of the things it knows, so we as individuals can continue on our course, change our course, improve our course, or accept our course. It is up to us as individuals to decide how we want to achieve our goals. We can listen to our dreams and know what will happen if we continue on the course we are on at the time, or if we don't like what the outcome may be, we have the option to change our course, by changing our attitude.

What we have been in the past, whether in past lives, or pre-existence, will effect what we are doing in the present. What we do in the present will effect what we will gain in the future, whether it is future lives or life after death. All of these lives are intertwined and effect each other.

Dreams have a lot to do with Quantum Physics. In Quantum Physics, consciousness travels faster than the speed of light. If that is so, then consciousness can travel into the future or the past, depending on what direction it chooses to go. If you consider your existence the center of a wheel and all you experience in the past or future, spokes of the wheel, rather than just a straight line followed in chronological order, you can see how consciousness can zap out to any given time, from your here and now, by choosing which spoke it wishes to zap out on. So in a sense, life is a circle without beginning or end, and everything in that circle is experience, all effecting the center of that circle which is Soul.

Each time sequence, or spoke, in the wheel is only real if it is focused on by the conscious mind, but the conscious mind can only focus on the center of the wheel which is your here and now experience. Therefore the sub conscious mind, or inner awareness has the job of traveling out to all these existence's and experiences to keep them all in order according to how the center of the wheel is progressing. If the center of the wheel is not in accordance with the outer spokes, it effects the balance of the wheel and how it progresses. It is not necessarily important what you do in all of the existence's or experiences you have, but how you are responding to the experience and what kind of attitude you come out with as a result. Your dreams tell you how you are responding to your everyday experiences and how they connect with all your past experiences, and therefore, how they will affect your future experiences.

Experience, or life, is made up of vibrations, which vibrate at different speeds. The higher the vibration, the more evolved the experience is. Because, like music, if you change the vibrations, it will change the pitch of the sound, and therefore change the melody. The lower the vibration the deeper the tone. The higher the tone, the more pleasant the melody seems to sound. But if it gets too high, it becomes uncomfortable to the ear, because our body is not used to vibrating at such high tones. Anything that falls below your vibration is uncomfortable to you and anything that vibrates higher that your vibrations is also uncomfortable to you. Dreams help you even out the vibrations of your experiences, and also raise your own vibrations, so eventually you will learn to vibrate at the same rate as God. Or in other words, be able to go to where ever it is that God dwells. If our vibration is not the same as God's vibration, we would feel uncomfortable in God's space.

Our experience is what determines our vibration, and our vibration is what determines how close to God we can get. So if the purpose of life is to get back to God in the end, and to do that we must raise our vibrations, then dreams are for us to recognize what vibrations we are on, and whether those vibrations will achieve the outcome we desire. (If you do not believe in God, consider that tapping into our inner-self will still help us balance out our life experiences.)

As experience is created by vibrations, each experience creates the next experience, by the way it is vibrating. If the vibration stays the same, we can pretty much predict what the next experience is likely to be. The same as the last experience! If we want our experiences to improve, we need to see how the other experiences are effecting our lives, and this is what dreams do for us. It measures our experiences and how they vibrate, then predicts what the next experience is likely to be if we continue on the same vibrations as before. It never tells us what the future will be. It only tells us what the future will most likely be if we do not change our direction of actions, attitudes, or beliefs. It tells us this in the symbolism of the dream and warns us of outcomes if we persist in going in the direction we are headed.

The other aspect of dreams is to inform us of past experiences we tend to forget, and show us how those experiences are effecting our present life. Now this can be past life experiences, or experiences of the past in this life. We can also dream of future experiences, which show us how all these experiences will affect our future life, and how that future life is actually affecting the present one.

If you think of life as an over lay, such as used in making animated cartoons, everything is actually happening at once. You can see through each overlay, into the next picture. If you change any of the overlays on any level, it affects the whole picture. The first drawing can affect the picture as much as the last one. The idea is to get all the drawings to harmonize and if one is a little off, you can flip to that drawing and change it even if it was drawn in another sequence of the whole project. Thus, we can change our overlays of life by going back and readjusting our attitude about the events that took place at the time. Dreams show us how readjusting our attitudes are effecting the whole picture!

Different types of Dreams

While we only seem to differentiate between pleasant dreams, and nightmares, there are acutely more types of dreams than just those two. There are past life experience dreams. Future experience or future life dreams. There are symbolic dreams. There are astral projection dreams. There are dreams that we knowingly create, and dreams that we create unknowingly. There are spiritual instruction dreams. There are transport dreams, where we travel in the dream state to other places, planets, or to communicate with other beings or aliens. There are dreams that we use to communicate with the dead, or are given instructions about those who have passed on, or will soon return in an incarnate body. There are dreams, where we actually exchange souls in our body with another who chooses to continue with our experience because we do not chose to continue our experience, and the dreams leading up to the actual exchange are our communications with the soul that agrees to exchange places with us. (These are rare and are what are considered "walk-ins", and can also happen at the death of one person and the near death of another.) There are dreams where we meet with other people that we plan to meet in the physical and set up the situation to create that meeting. There are probably even more types of other dreams than I have mentioned, but these are the ones I am aware of.

Sometimes it is difficult to tell one dream from another, but there are small sighs that can give you some clue as to what kind of dream you are having at the time. I will go through each type of dream, and explain to you what to be most aware of, as to the best of my knowledge or experience.

Past life experience dreams. These dreams are like de ja`vu. You seem to think you have dreamed them before, but you can't remember when. Everything in them seems very familiar to you, but you know that the experience never happened in this life. You may have the same dream several times and each time the dream impresses you because it is so familiar to you. These dreams you may think are omens of disaster or good luck, depending on the dream. The reason for this feeling is because it is something that has happened to you before that you have not resolved, or have resolved and you are strengthening the lesson from the experience.

For instance, my sister kept having a dream about a chandelier falling in flames on a big oak dining room table and starting the house on fire. Because she had this dream so many times, she started to worry that it meant that her house might start on fire and the chandelier might have something to do with it. The dream was so real to her, that sometimes when she woke up she could even smell the smoke. She worried so much that her husband took the chandelier apart and examined it for shorts in the wiring, but nothing serious was wrong. She still had the dream.

It was several years later when she had a past life recall that she learned that she had lived during the Civil War, and the home she was living in was accidentally set on fire by her mother. As she roused herself from sleep and ran into the upstairs hall, the chandelier fell onto the table in flames. The memory was so impressive to her that she had not completely lost it from that past life. Also many things that had happened to her in that life had not been resolved, and the dream was reminding her that those things were still effecting her attitude in her present life.

Future experience dreams. These dreams are a little harder to detect, because you don't always realize that they are future experiences, until they happened after you dreamed them. These dreams you may have several times also, only instead of thinking, you remember the incident, and it feeling very familiar to you, you feel frightened by them, if they are bad experiences, or enlightened by them, if they are good experiences and have a sense of anticipation. You have a sense of dread if they are frightening dreams. The other thing about them, is that they seem very real and do not feel like a dream.

All dreams, even dreams depicting the future, are derived from the events taking place at the time of the dream itself, and the futuristic aspect is that whatever you are doing at the time, of the dream, the dream indicates how it is affecting your reality at the time and as a result, how it will ultimately affect your future also. This will be better understood when I describe some of the dreams I had. What was happening at the time of the dream, and how the dream became part of my future reality.

Astral projection dreams. These dreams are usually very pleasant. In them, we are usually flying, or trying to fly. We sometimes bounce and our body seems weightless. The more energy we are putting into trying to stay off the ground indicates our lack of inexperience in using the astral body.

The astral body is a physical body (within or without our own physical body) that vibrates at a higher level than the physical. Therefore, the matter that the body is made up of is a tighter form and can actually go through physical forms, such as walls etc. because lower vibrations are a looser form of solidity. We seem to think it is the other way around and that ghosts or astral bodies are made up of air or light, when in truth, we are the illusion of from and everything higher in vibration is closer to pure God energy which all physical form is a part of.

Because the astral body is finer and lighter, it is not effected by earthly confines and gravity and solid forms have no effect on it.

Therefore, when we are in the astral form, which separates from our physical form we feel a lightness. However, we tend to think that we are still in the physical form, while we are dreaming and are amazed that we are flying. The moment we start to think of our physical body, or something happens to bring us back to the physical awareness, such as having a hard time breathing, or an arm falling asleep, our astral body zaps back into the physical, whether we like it or not. Sometimes, when this happens we get a very impressive sense of feeling heavy, after having such a weightless feeling prior to returning to the physical.

Also, if we mentally and emotionally relate more to our physical body than our Astral body, the first time we become aware of "floating out", we experience a physical "bumping into the ceiling" and the falling back into the physical.

Along with Astral projection dreams, you may experience **Astral instruction dreams.** In these dreams, you may receive answers to puzzling questions you may have been having. You may create inventions, get new ideas for books, or be able to resolve a problem that has been plaguing you for a long time. When you have these dreams, you feel enlightened about whatever it is that has been bothering, and you suddenly come up with a solution to the problem.

An example of this type of dream is one experienced by the man who invented the White sewing machine. Mr. White was having problems trying to figure out how to make the thread go through the needle to pick up the bobbin thread. Most needles have the hole in the end of the needle and is pulled thorough the cloth. However, that that was not feasible with the sewing machine. One night, Mr. White had a dream that he was captured by cannibals, who told him that he had two hours to figure out this problem concerning the needle, and if he didn't do it, they were going to eat him. They put him in a hut, and for two hours, he thought and thought but couldn't come up with a solution. Finally, they came, got him, and proceeded to get him ready to eat. They all stood around him brandishing their spears and then he noticed something very strange about the spears. They all had a point at the end of them, but in the middle of that point, there was a hole and then he knew what the solution to the problem was. Put the hole for the thread at the point of the needle! He then woke up and used this to solve the problem he was having.

Communication dreams, are also a form of Astral dreams. In these dreams, you see people you know, or don't know, but you feel like it is really happening and that you are talking to them. When you wake up you are surprised that it was a dream you were having because it seemed so real.

An example of this sort of dream is one I had several years ago about my cousin. As I grew up, I had a cousin that I was very close to, and our younger years were spent together a lot. His mother was my mother's sister, and his father was my father's brother, which made us double cousins and practically brothers and sisters! After about the age twenty-five, I never saw him again because I was married and moved out of the state he lived in. I always felt a certain loss at not being around him, yet he never seemed too excited about my company. It was all I could do to get him to write me when we were young, and so I never attempted to get him to do it as we grew older!

When I was about 35, I had this dream that I saw my cousin. I actually thought it was real, and that I was truly visiting him! I told him how much I missed him and how glad I was to see him again. We talked of all the good times we had together as children, and I thoroughly enjoyed my visit with him. When I woke up I was so surprised that it had been a dream, because it seemed so real! The next night I dreamed I saw him again. This time I said to him, "You know, I had the strangest dream about you last night!" I went on to tell him about the dream, and how real it all seemed. Then when I woke up again, I was so surprised that this was yet another dream and it really hadn't happened! The next night, I dreamed about him again. This time I said to him, "I don't know whether this is a dream or not, but just in case it isn't, you know I have been dreaming about you lately!" This was most likely an astral dream where I needed to have some sort of contact with my cousin and his astral form, agreed to meet with mine, since we couldn't do it in the physical form.

Transport dreams. These dreams are a lot like astral dreams, but can be in other forms of the physical or spiritual bodies. (We have several forms of bodies within our physical body, each vibrating at a higher rate than the others do. Spirit vibrates at the same level as God, and we may transfer to Spirit if our dreaming takes us into a Spiritual awareness.) In these dreams, we usually are aware of guides, directing our experience in the dream. We may perceive that we are talking to higher beings or beings from other planets. Sometimes we find ourselves in other parts of the world talking to friends that live there, or total strangers to us, that we have the feeling that we know. These dreams may also be linked with **Spiritual instruction dreams.** The difference in some spiritual instruction dreams, from transport dreams, is that the Spiritual instructor comes to you and instructs you, rather than you going to them for instruction. In these dreams you have a feeling of peace and love emanated from the person in your dream. The dream may inspire you and help you overcome some conflict in your life, such as losing a loved one or overcoming a traumatic experience.

Communicating with the dead. In these dreams, someone in your life who has passed on, may come to you in the dream and talk with you or give you instruction. Sometimes it is a feeling of their presences, rather than seeing them in your dream. Sometimes they take on faces of other people, but you know that it is them. If the person in your dream looks the same age as they were when they died, then it is most likely a communication dream, but if they are younger, it is most likely a past remembrance dream that had something to do with the concepts that they stood for in your life. If someone else presents them to you and they look younger, it is usually an indication that the person who has died is about to be reintroduced to the physical and you are being informed of this upcoming event.

Meeting people in dreams prior to meeting them in the physical. Sometimes we set up meetings with people who will be important to our spiritual growth, or physical experience here on earth. In the dream state we set up plans that we wish our lives to follow. There are so many probabilities to choose from, that our inner consciousness, which is traveling faster than the speed of light, has the job of zapping into each probability to see how compatible it will be with the rest of our experiences. Many other people from past existence's who may have some part to play in this existence are always ready to take part in our "play", if we choose it. Therefore, we can decide in the dream state which of these people, who already live on the earth at the same time that we do, will be allowed to take part in our experience. We set up ways to meet them in the dream state and we both agreed on doing so, long before we ever do meet. These dreams are difficult to remember, and are usually not remembered until after we meet the person decided on in the dream. We get the feeling that either we have met them before, or a feeling of de ja`vu when we do meet them.

Exchanging souls. The exchanging of the souls does not really happen in a dream. What does happen is that the two souls who have agreed to do the exchanging, meet in the dream state and agree to the exchange. During some dreams the soul that wishes to take over the experience of the one in the physical, occupies that body for short periods of time to get used to the physical before actually changing with the other. This is usually only done, when one soul has lost all desire to continue its experience in that particular life, but knows the penalty of committing suicide. The "walk in" soul is one who does not want to go through the hassle of childhood, and evolving its awareness. It usually has a particular mission to accomplish and wants a means to do it. One soul will never take over a physical body, unless the soul possessing the body agrees to exchange places with it. Two souls do not exchange physical bodies for different experiences though. One soul has to be bodiless, and desire a body. The other has to be willing to leave the body it possesses and start over from soul, again. The soul entering the body takes on the memories of that person. The only thing that is different is the attitude and ambitions of the soul entering the body that is turned over to it. Another means of exchange, is when one person dies unexpectedly and has not finished what it has planned for that particular existence. If it can find another soul who is close to death, because it has no desire to remain on earth, but the body could survive if the soul was willing, they may agree to exchange places. It is still agreed upon by both souls, and may also be accomplished in the dream state, or instantaneously at the time of death, and near death of the individuals involved.

Symbolic dreams. This is the most common kind of dreaming and is the one I am going to explain in more depth in this book. The Symbolic dream is a series of incidents tied together, that may or may not make any sense to the dreamer. The dream itself actually does make sense when it is being experienced, but only to the inner consciousness. Because it is in the language of the inner, that language has to be put into pictures or symbols that are more native to the outer consciousness. Because of this, there are some gaps in the fluency of what is taking place. It seems perfectly natural while the dream is taking place, but upon awaking and remembering, the scenes do not always fit together as naturally as the dream seemed to be doing when in progress. The reason for this is that while the message of the dream may follow in a smooth inner expression, the symbols used in deciphering the message, may have little relation to each other. For instance, if you made up a code and used names of animals in place of words, when you read the code, it would make no sense at all. The person who had the key would see the message, but the person who didn't have the key would just see a long list of names of animals! Because the outer consciousness, has forgotten the pure language of the inner, it would never be able to understand any of its dreams if that language was not transformed. Because we believe the illusion of our reality, if the truth of our reality is depicted in the dream form, it would be too much of a shock to our psyche and the dreaming would do us little good. Our inner always knows the meaning of a dream whether it is changed into symbols or not, but it would do the outer consciousness little good, if it could not understand the dream also.

Even though we may think the dream makes no sense, the very fact that it is put in symbols that make us stop and wonder about the dream, serves a purpose. Because the outer has now been shaken a little, and it becomes more aware of the dreaming self, it may start to question its own reality and try to find answers.

In this short book, I hope to help the reader find some of the answers to the meaning of their dreams. The methods I use seem to work for most dreams, even if they are not necessarily a symbolic dream. Even if you are dreaming of past experiences or future experiences, or communicating with the dead, there are still messages in the very act of doing that. The symbols I plan to show you will help you discover why you are dreaming of the past, or what messages the dead are trying to impart

SYMBOLS

Everything in your dream is a SYMBOL. The emotions you feel about the dream, tell you how you are responding to the symbol. While all symbols of every dream, whether it is your dream or the dream of someone else, are the same in every instance, the relationship of that symbol to the individual is what makes the dream unique to that individual. This is why dreaming of a horse to one person, cannot mean the same to another person dreaming of a horse. The relationship that each person has to horses, changes the meaning of the dream. This is the reason I feel dream dictionaries cannot do a good job, because relationships to various things in life differ so much from person to person. So how can you apply a blanket statement made concerning dreams about horses to every person who ever dreams about horses?

In Symbols, it is not the horse that is the symbol, but animals in general. Then if you know what your relationship to the animal you are dreaming of is, it tells you how that symbol relates to you personally.

So now, I will give you a list of the most common things found in dreams, and what they symbolize. If for some reason I do not cover some of the symbols you may have had in your dreams, refer to the symbols mentioned and see how they are derived and you will probably be able to derive a symbol for other things in your dream not mentioned here.

Animals. Any time you dream about animals, insects, or monsters, or any other living things that are not people, either real or imagined, it represents **Challenges**. The relationship you have to the animal dreamed about, will tell you what kind of challenge it represents to you. What the animal is doing, will tell you the seriousness of the challenge. What you are doing to or with the animal tells you how you are handling the challenge. What happens to that animal at your hands, or to you at the animal's hands, tells you what you do with the challenge or what the challenge has done or is doing to you. The emotions that you feel while dealing with the animal, tells you how you feel emotionally about the challenge in real life. The size of the animal tells you how big of a challenge it is. Sometimes an animal that should be small becomes large in your dream and visa versa. How dangerous the animal, whether large or small, tells you the danger of the challenge, regardless of the size.

So, if you were dreaming about a horse, and you feared horses in real life, that dream would represent more of a challenge to you than to a person who works with horses every day and loves it! If you fear the horses, but in the dream, you get on its back, this could indicate that you are climbing up and taking on a challenge in spite of your fear of that challenge. If you don't fear horses and are very familiar with them, it would mean that the challenge is a familiar one that you deal with daily. If you have never had horses, but love them and would like to have one, it would mean that it is a challenge that you would love to have and deal with. If you used to have horses, but don't any more, it would mean that the challenge is one that you used to deal with and could deal with again. I could go on and on with different scenarios of what dreaming of a horse could mean about your challenge, but I hope you have gotten the picture by now.

The next step is to see what it is that the horse is doing. Is it just walking along slow and easy, or running away with you, or trying to buck you off? Is it trying to trample you or kick you, or running away from you so you have to chase it? Is it chasing you or are you chasing it? Whatever the horse is doing represents what your challenge is doing in real life.

In the end, who gets the upper hand in the dream? Does the horse get you off it's back? Do you ever get on its back? Do you stay on its back? Do you tame it, or does it get the best of you? This tells how you will deal with the challenge or how the challenge will end up dealing with you.

If it were a monster, that eats you up, then you can pretty much figure that you have a monster of a challenge that is going to eat you up. If it is a monster that you whip into submission, it would indicate that you have a monster of a challenge, but you will end up wearing it down in the end.

The number of the animals can indicate the numbers of challenges, but it can also have deeper meaning, since numbers have a meaning in themselves. I will give you the meaning of numbers later in the list of symbols.

If it were little insects crawling all over you, this would indicate a lot of irritating challenges that may or may not be much of a problem, depending on what happens to those little insects in the dream. Do you swat them or do they turn into black widow spiders?

Books. Books are a place where information is stored. Dreaming of books indicates your search for answers and the type of books show where your concerns lie. If it is a religious book, it is a source of comfort, or discovering answers to spiritual questions. The feeling you get in the dream about the book expresses whether you were able to find the answers you were looking for. How the book relates to the rest of your dream will also give you more insight on its meaning.

Buildings. Buildings represent **security**, or that which protects you from the outside world in some way. A house would represent family security. A church, temple synagogue, etc., represents religious or spiritual security. An office building, or a place of work, such as a factory, etc., would represent job security. A store would represent security you get from your buying power. A bank would represent financial security. A school would represent the security you get from your knowledge or lack of knowledge, depending on the dream. A hospital represents your security of health. A theater or stadium could mean the security you get from your leisure time or entertainments. A restaurant the security you get from eating, which could also mean food for thought or growth not only in body, but also in spirit.

The condition of the building represents the condition of the security. If it is run down it would mean the same thing for your security. If it is on fire, your security may be in danger, but fire also represents cleansing or purification, so the danger may only be temporary until the fire has transformed the security. If the building is large, it would indicate the size of your security, and so on.

What happens to the building in relation to the dream shows you what happens or may happen to your security, if you don't change your ways or attitude. How you feel about what happens, shows you your attitude concerning your security and what is happening to it in the dream.

Colors. If you dream in color, the colors that you are aware of in your dream usually have certain meanings along with the dream. If it is in color, but nothing about the color stands out in your mind, it is probably not that crucial to the dream.

RED, is an emotional color. Usually, the emotion of anger, rage or excitement. It can also have a sexual meaning too.

ORANGE, is physical, and deals with physical limitations.

MAGENTA, is individuality, and independence.

YELLOW, means joy, and mental capacity.

TAN, is also physical, but rather than limitations, it is physical translating of messages to the mental.

GREEN, using mental powers. It can also stand for envy.

BLUE, is nurturing, and also a form of power. (Placing a blue light around something is a form of protection, or healing.)

PINK, is health or new life. It could indicate pregnancy or the feeling of youth.

PURPLE, is a royal color and could also have political implications.

VIOLET, is the highest vibration of color, next to white. It indicates the psychic powers and ability to communicate on a psychic level.

LAVENDER, is imagination, fantasy, escape of reality. It reaches into other realms of reality, which you may consider illusion, but could very well be closer to reality than you know! It represents high unreachable ideals.

BROWN, is earth and or could indicate muddy or confused ideas.

CRYSTAL, is healing.

WHITE, is purity and the highest vibration, being the vibration of God, and the combination of all color.

BLACK, is the absence of color and darkness to the soul. It is not necessarily a bad color, but describes the affect that black may play in "black concepts" or someone in your dream may consider as a "black concept" depending on the dream, but it may not mean that the concept is actually black, but only you or other's opinion of it is black.

Clothes. Clothes are what cover you and represent what you want the outside world to see you as, so it would represent how you **represent yourself**. However, the clothes fit you is how your representation to others truly fits you. If you are wearing no clothes, this indicates that you are showing your true self to others and are not trying to misrepresent yourself in any way. How you feel about the clothes you are wearing tells how you feel about the way you represent yourself to others. How you feel about your nudity in your dream, tells how you feel about showing your true self to others. Clothes and colors have a tie in that whatever the color of clothes you see yourself wearing in your dream will indicate some of the ways you show yourself to others, during the time period that the dream takes place.

All dreams, even dreams depicting the future, are derived from the events taking place at the time of the dream itself. The futuristic aspect is that whatever you are doing at the time of the dream, the dream indicates how it is effecting your reality at the time, and as a result how it will ultimately affect your future also. This will be better understood when I describe some of the dreams I had, what was happening at the time of the dream, and how the dream became part of my future reality.

Death. Death in dreams does not mean literal death. It only means **change.** When something or somebody dies in a dream, whether it is you or someone else, it does not necessarily indicate that someone is going to die. It only means the death, or change of the concept that the person represents. (see people) The death of an animal is the death of a challenge, or challenges conquered, or changed. If your mother dies, it may indicate that the concepts your mother had about you are starting to die and something else is taking their place, or that your own concepts of mother is changing. If you are the one dying, it is the death of your own ego, and a change of concepts about yourself.

If you are killing or causing the death of someone or something, you are changing or killing other concepts and challenges that, the person or animal represents in your life. If they are trying to kill you, they or their concepts are trying to kill the concept of yourself. How you feel about the death in your dream, tell you how you feel about that concept dying or changing. How you respond to the death, tells how you will respond to the change that takes place as those concepts or challenges die. If you are trying to kill yourself, it indicates that there is something about your own concepts or ego you are trying to change, or kill.

If however, two or more people dream of a death of a friend or family at the same time and especially when they see each other in the dream surrounding the death whether they know each other or not, and in comparing the dreams, they are pretty much the same, this could be the indication that the person dreamed about could be dying or is about to have ill health or a sudden devastating change in their lives, depending on other contents of the dream. (Even if you dream about something that ends up happening in the future, the symbols of the dream shows you how this will affect you, when the incident happens.)

Fire. Fire **purifies**, or changes the structure of things. If you dream about fire, whatever is being consumed by the fire is being changed, and in a sense purified. It is the method of forging steel to strengthen it, or cauterizing a wound to stop the bleeding. The method is painful, but strengthens in the end.

Flowers. Flowers represent nature and love. It can be human love and possibly God love depending on how the flowers fit into the dream. The color of the flowers may play a part in the meaning of the dream as well.

Food: When you dream of food, it is an indication of food for thought and fills you with understanding of the situation at hand that the dream is dealing with.

Groups: A large group of people would represent what that group of concepts stood for. A church congregation may indicate religious concepts. A class of students could mean educational concepts. People on the street, could indicate the concepts of society

Music: Music represents harmony in life. and what is happening concerning the music in your dream will indicate what kind of harmony or working well with your life experiences, your path is taking.

Nightmares: Whenever you have a very frightening dream, it is actually a good dream. It is your inner self, trying to shake up the outer self to make an important impression on you. If the "bad" dream (as you see it) is repeated, it indicates that you have not responded to the warnings of the last dream, and you are being reminded to pay attention to the symbols in the dream so you will be prepared for events in your life. These sorts of dreams are buffers for us so when actual incidents happen to us, whether harsh or exciting, the physic self will already be braced for the incident and it won't be as hard on the physical or mental self.

Numbers. Numbers, like colors have separate meanings for each number. However, only the numbers from 1 to 9 have a meaning, and any combinations of numbers need to be broken down by adding them up, such as 33 would be 3+3=6 or taking them separately, such as 33 is really two 3s. However, some numbers are not broken down, and 33 is one of them. 11, 22, and 33, always remain because they have a meaning all their own. All the other combination of numbers can be added up or separated. This would have to be at the digression of the dreamer, depending on the feeling you seem to get from the number represented in your dream. If you actually see the number written in your dream, it may have a different meaning than seeing six sheep wandering down the road, and discovering the meaning of what the number six has to do with it all.

If the number is a telephone number, and you remember it, or an address, or a page in a book, etc., the rest of the dream has to be taken into consideration before deciding just what the number means.   You may have to discover all the meanings that the number might represent, and see how each meaning fits into your dream. Somewhere it should make sense to you when you find the right meaning to that numbers.

Because of the large aspects that numbers cover, and the many meanings of numbers, if you have a lot of dreams with numbers that seem important to you, you may want to get a book on numerology, and perhaps a Tarot book, both which deal with numbers and the meaning of numbers.

I will give you a simplified list of the meanings of numbers to help you in the beginning.

ONE, represents independence, a single eye to God, the beginning.

TWO, partnership, balance, duality, equality, love.

THREE, creation, family, building, the trinity, fertility, expansion.

FOUR, cooperation, pulling together, evening out, reaping what you sew, building.

FIVE, risk, pushing to the limit, exploring new territory, stretching, achieving, vacillating.

SIX, content, feeling of arrival, a breath of relief, feeling sure of self, getting beyond the risk.

SEVEN, a God number, spirituality, idealism, wisdom.

EIGHT, financial stability, accomplishments, retirement, achievement.

NINE, reaching the end, the last step before beginning again, evolving, peace of mind, preparing for higher achievements.

11, 22, 33, are all spiritual numbers, and are indications of the soul. They are highly evolved and represent spiritual teachers. 33 is the indication of complete physical achievement in overcoming physical limitations and going on to spiritual attainment.

People. People are not really people in your dream, unless you are dreaming of a past life, or communicating with someone specifically. Even when they do represent real people, there is a symbol connected to it. People represent **concepts.** The importance of the person in the dream to you represents the importance of that concept that the person represents.

For example, if you are dreaming of your mother, father, grandparents, etc., it would indicate the concepts that those people stood for in your life. A mother might be a nurturing concept, unless your mother was never nurturing. The older the person is in your dream, the older the concept. A grandparent may be an old tried and true concept that was taught to you by your grandparents, or something that your grandparents believed in themselves. A baby would be a brand new concept that has just come into your life, or the concepts you feel about giving birth, or caring for children or the concepts of family and raising children, etc.

Pregnancy: Being pregnant in the dream indicates a concept being developed and giving birth is the same as giving birth to that concept.

Spiritual Beings: If you see angles, or God, (or you think it is God) or religious leaders, it is the concepts that those angles represent, or that the religious leaders believe in.

Radio, television, telephone, Internet: Any form of communication, are symbols for communication or how you are hearing and perceiving communications from others. A radio would most likely indicate your ability to listen correctly or how you are hearing things, since radios are only listened to and you can't talk back to them. A telephone is a form of listening and speaking, as is the Internet. They indicate what is happening with your two-way communication in your life, where talking personally face to face with someone, would be more about communicating concepts, or understanding other's concepts. A television shows how you see and hear things that are happening around you. Whatever is happing on the television shows how you are hearing and seeing things, but not necessarily communicating with the things you are hearing and seeing since you usually can't communicate with a television.

Religious Figures. Religious leaders, either alive or dead, or spiritual masters, etc., in a dream, is also an indication that this dream has spiritual messages to impart and that you should pay close attention to what is happening in the dream. It would also indicate your religious concepts concerning what is happening in the dream.

Repetitious Dreams: When a dream is repeated throughout your life, or for several days or months, etc., it is an issue that you are dealing with or need to resolve and the dream is reminding you that you have not worked with that issue and need to pay attention to it. When you have resolved the problem or issue, the dream will stop, unless it is a prophetic dream or past life dream, which is either for-warning you of something, or reliving a past experience that needs to be dealt with.

Sex: Sexual dreams are actually an indication of spiritual evolution. When you are in the nude it is an indication that you are being honest and open about who you are. When you are in the nude with others you are being honest about your concepts of others or concepts in general and the person you are having sex with in the dream indicates your acceptance of the concepts that they represent to you. Our connection to others and other concepts is part of growing and seeing our complete connection with everyone and everything in this physical existence. As we discover our connection with others, it is actually a spiritual awakening and the sexual dreams, informs us that we are one-step closer to spiritual understanding. When an actual climax is experienced during the dream, it indicates that we have accomplished one spiritual phase in our growth and are embarking on the next phase of understanding. Just having a climax during sleep with no dream surrounding it, probably does not apply.

However, if you are in the nude or having sex in a dream and you are embarrassed or upset by it, it indicates that you still have a long way to go in order to feel completely spiritually comfortable around others, or your spiritual communication with others. It could be that the person in your dream, who makes you feel uncomfortable or embarrassed, represents concepts that are holding you back from your spiritual growth or openness to others. It can show your lack of trust when you are open with others as well, depending on the concepts surrounding you in the dream. (people you know or don't know)

Shapes: Different shapes such as triangles, stars, circles, squares, etc., in a dream have their own meaning, depending on the shapes. Like colors, or numbers, each is different. Usually shapes are noticed as objects in your dream that you seem to feel are important, when you are dreaming, or when you awake you are very aware of the shapes that you saw and they have impressed you somehow.

CIRCLES, indicate love or eternity, since it has no beginning or end.

STARS, are religious or spiritual symbols, such as the Star of David or the star of Bethlehem. People look to the stars for direction, or stars fill them with wonder and are a mystery.

TRINGLES also can have religious indications. They are the shape of the pyramids. They are also a form of the Star of David, superimposed on each other with one reversed. They have three points, which could stand for the trinity. (Father, Son, Holy Ghost)

SQUARES stand for constructive things. Blocks are used to build house etc.

HEXAGONS are many sided and can indicate that there are more sides to the situation than meets the eyes. Also bees have hexagon squares in their hive and they are a part of nature and very symmetrical, so they can also indicate perfection of nature or God, since they have six sides and the world was (according to the bible) was formed in six days, or actually six steps. This will depend on how the shapes are used in your dream.

Sickness: Being sick in a dream or seeing someone else sick or in a hospital, indicates a healing dream. Not so much physical healing though it could be, but emotional and spiritual healing. Whatever the sick person's relationship to you in your dream will help you determine what this sickness represents. The hospital would be your security in health, but could also indicate spiritual or mental health. Other people being sick could represent concepts of those people and how it effects your healing or remaining sick.

Teaching: If you are teaching something in a dream it is a form of sharing your talents or yourself with others and the dream shows you how you are doing that or attempting to do that in your waking life.

Tools: When tools are being used in a dream, and this can be anything used to do something with, it indicates the means by which you accomplish certain tasks. Whatever the task that the dream is dealing with, such as fixing a car, could indicate the tools used to create or fix your outer motivation, (see transportation) or what has influenced that motivation. The surrounding elements in the dream will indicate what part the tools play in the dream.

Transportation. Any form of transportation, or movement, represents **motivation.** The mode of transportation tells you the type of motivation it represents. There is outside motivation, and inside motivation, and there is a combination of both. If the form of transportation is powered by any means other than your own power, it is a form of outside motivation.

For example, a car, boat, train, plane, motorcycle, etc. are all powered by an engine. Even though you my guide that means of transportation, it takes an outside form of power to move it. Therefore, it would indicate outside motivation. If the form of transportation is a bicycle, skateboard, skates, paddle board, skies, or any form that you have to physically participate in to get it to move, it is a combination of outside motivation, (the vehicle itself) and inside motivation. (the person making the vehicle move) If the form of transportation is only physical, running, walking, swimming, crawling, etc. it is a form of inside motivation, motivated by you and nothing else.

So if you are dreaming of being in a car, driving down the street, it indicates that some form of outside motivation is moving you in that direction. Where the car takes you tells you where the outside motivation will get you. How that car gets you there, will tell you how the progress to that point will be.

For instance, if the car gets you from one point to the other without much trouble, it means that the outside motivation does not seem to hinder you much. However, if the car is racing down a hill, and there are no brakes on the car and try as you might, you can't stop it and you are afraid you are going to go off a cliff or crash in some way, this is showing you that the outside motivation is out of control and may cause a major "crash" in your life.

If you are in a boat, (outside motivation) powered by a motor, and it is not getting you to your destination, so you jump out and start swimming, (inside motivation) it would show that the outside motivation you were using was not working, so you chose to use inside motivation to accomplish your goals. However, jumping into the water, would indicate jumping into emotions, in order to use your inner motivation to get you to your goal.

If someone else is driving the car that you are in, it is the concept that the person driving represents, guiding outside motivation that you have no control over at all. Whatever is happening in that car in the dream is how that concept directs the motivation that drives you.

Trees. Trees are **spiritual** and healing. It indicates **Nature** affecting your reality. Whatever you are doing around the trees, or in the trees, etc, will indicate what the effect of spiritual influences and nature are having on you.

Trips or Traveling: Seeing yourself on a trip or seeing someone else go on a trip is a way of showing you where you are going in this life and how you are getting there. Other people are concepts you have concerning those people and the trip they are taking is where those concepts are taking you or how they are influencing you on your own journey in this life.

Up and Down: Whenever you are traveling up, in any way, whether it is flying, climbing, driving, etc. it is an indication of **evolving** closer to God. Going **down**, would mean losing ground, or **un-evolving.** The feeling you get as you climb up or down, indicate how you are responding to evolving or un-evolving. If you are using inside motivation to get there, such as climbing a mountain, for example, it would indicate that inside motivation was the means of your own evolvement. If you are driving a car up a hill or mountain, etc., then outside motivation is getting you there. So by the same means, if this car is plunging down a hill, it means outside motivation is the source of your un-evolvement and something needs to be done about it. If you are flying without means of any vehicle, it is the evolving of your astral abilities, and whether your efforts are taking you up or down is how you are achieving your astral levels. **Falling** is also a form of **down** but indicates a faster rate of descending. Meaning you are suddenly losing ground, and the fear of landing and ending your life.(or experience) Life is eternal, and therefore, even if you fall from grace, or fall in your effort to evolve, you can never hit bottom. Therefore, even if you actually see yourself hit bottom in your dream, it does not mean that you will actually die! The experience may be shocking to you, and so shocking that you may choose to wake up before seeing yourself splat on the ground. It is only to show you that falling from all you have achieved is as bad as death itself and feared by all of us, for it takes us father from God and our striving to raise our vibrations in order to get closer to God. (or something higher than ourselves.)

Water.   Water represents **emotions**. Whatever form the water takes, tells you the type of emotions it represents. How you feel about the water, tells you how you feel about the emotions represented in your dream. What you are doing in, or out of the water, tells you your relationship to those emotions and how you are dealing with them. However deep the water, it is the depth of the emotions.

If, for example, the water is rough, it would indicate rough emotions. If it were calm then calm emotions are involved. If you can see to the bottom, the emotions are clear, but if it is muddy and murky, it means those kind of emotions are involved. If you are afraid of the water, then you are afraid of the emotions represented in the dream. If you leap into the water unafraid, than you are also leaping into your emotions the same way, whether they are, rough, murky, clear, etc. If you leap into the water, in spite of the fact that it scares you, you are willing to leap into frightening emotions. Whatever happens in the water indicates what will happen to you if you engulf yourself in those emotions. If you drown than your emotions may drown you also. If you fight against the current, than you are fighting against the current of your emotions in real life. If you think you are going to drown, but don't, then it indicates that in spite of your fears of drowning in your emotions, you will survive.

If you are in a boat in a river or lake, etc., it is outside motivation skimming you over the top of your emotions. You are not getting your feet wet, even though you are out in the middle of them all. If you are rowing the boat, there is some inside motivation pulling you through your emotions, but you are still safe from being pulled under, or even touching the emotions. If the boat sinks, then the outside motivation is not going to save you from those emotions, and your inside motivation will have to take over. If you willingly jump from the boat to swim, then your inner motivation will pull you through your emotions and you are willingly emerging in them. If the water carries you away, and you have no power over it, once you have jumped in, your inner motivation is not strong enough to save you from where the emotions will eventually take you. The emotions may take you to a good place, or a bad place, and that will indicate what your emotions are doing to you in real life.

Whoever else is swimming around with you in that river of emotions, or with you in the boat, or waiting for you on the shore, etc., are the concepts that you have about those emotions, or the motivation that keeps you from the emotions, or the concepts that remain away from the effect of those emotions, etc.

You can see, as we go along and combine all the symbols together in the dream that a reasonable meaning can be derived from all aspects of the dream, regardless of what is involved in the dream.

So if you take some of the other symbols, such as houses, and you see them being washed away in a storm, then you would know that emotions are washing away your securities. Or, if you see all of your friends bombarded by a title wave, you would know that all the concepts that those friends represent in your life are being pounded by overwhelming emotions.

Weather: Weather indicates forces beyond your control. They are not motivations, but are influences that indicate how outside forces or destiny may be affecting you. If the weather is stormy, it is a force that may seem dangerous, but like challenges, how you deal with the forces in your life, such as karma, destiny, missions in life, etc., are indicated by the symbols of the dream. If there is a rainbow involved after the bad weather in your dream, this is like the promise given to Noah, that in spite of the forces working against you, God is still there watching over you and all the colors of spiritual influences will always be there to help you evolve. If you fear the weather, then it indicates that you fear or do not understand where your destiny is taking you. If you are brave enough to face the storm, unshaken and unafraid, you are also facing life that way. Pleasant weather is your peace of mind and harmony with whatever your destiny or outside forces are.

Because some weather involves water, the water in the weather dream would indicate emotions, but emotions caused by outside forces and possibly karma. Snow could be frozen emotions or emotions that cover and disguise the real issue. Wind would indicate power that these outside forces have on you and the stronger the wind the stronger the power. Earthquakes would indicate changes that threaten you. It could only mean that to start fresh, you have to destroy the past structures in your life. Volcanoes can be linked with fire but are still outside forces or destinies that are bringing you to painful changes of purification. Lightening is a form of "shock" that outside forces are presenting to you and making you face.

Weight Loss or Gain: When weight is involved in a dream, such as seeing yourself or someone else heavier in a dream, or a lot lighter than in true life, it is an indication of the loss or gain of a burden. Other people, of course, are really concepts, so it could indicate a burden centered on the concept that the person represents to you, if it is someone else gaining or losing weight in your dream.

Wires: Wires, such as fence wires, wires in electrical fixtures, telephone wires, etc. connect thing together. Wires in your dream indicate how you or other things are connected together. Depending on what the wire is for in your dream, indicates what kind of connection it is depicting. Such as wires in a radio may describe the way you connect things together that you hear, or the source of your ability to listen to things may have to do with your own connectedness to that thing, etc. Fence wires might represent what you see as a connection to the boundaries that you won't go beyond in your dealing in life.

This list constitutes the majority of symbols most likely seen in dreams. However, there are always unusual things unaccounted for that may pop up in dreams which may not fit into anything that I have mentioned. If you give it proper thought and try to see the connection that those objects in your dream may have to real life, or what those objects mean to you personally, it will help you discover your own symbolic meaning to the objects or situations in your dream.

STEPS TO TAKE TO ANALYZE DREAMS FROM EXAMPLES OF DREAMS AND THEIR MEANING.

In this section, I will give you some examples of dreams I have had or other people have had, which I have analyzed, the steps I went through to do so.

First let's look at some simple dreams:

Little Bunny Rabbits:

A girlfriend of mine in college told me of a dream that she had. She said that she had all these cages full of little bunny rabbits. Having the pets seemed pleasant to her, but the constant care it took ran her ragged. She saw herself running from cage to cage to take care of them and never had time to do anything else.

Meaning:

In her real life, she was taking college classes that she didn't have to take yet, but she wanted to cram as much into her schedule as she could in order to get a lot of little simple classes behind her. Also, she was staying after class to do extra work on some of the subjects she was taking. As a result, she didn't have much time for her boyfriend or anything else.

The dream was telling her that her classes were challenges, like little bunny rabbits. While they appeared harmless enough and were courses that she was interested in, she had to give them care, the same way she would have to care for little rabbits. It would take all of her time. She could to it, but did she want to spend all of her time feeding challenges, and not have time for more important things?

My house dreams:

I have had several dreams about houses. In these dreams, the houses were old and familiar, or we were going to buy a house and when we went to look at it, the house had many rooms and I kept finding unusual rooms, or more rooms than I remembered, or the house had belonged to a family member and I kept finding new rooms that I didn't know were there.

Meaning:

These dreams indicate the constant changing in my home security and always looking for (or trying to buy) more security in my home life. However, I gain my security from old traditions, or long for ways that things were done in my own home life. However, I kept discovering that there is more to security than a simple house would represent. I keep finding more rooms that I never knew about, which means I am finding new ways of creating the security I strive for and how I feel about the rooms when I find them, is how I feel about these new ways of making my life more secure.

Premonitions of my divorce.

Now I will take you systematically through a dream I had when I was married, but I did not know what the dream meant until five years after I had the dream, since I did not know how to analyze dreams at that time.

I dreamed that my two girls, Chandelle and Marni, were playing down by the creek. (at the time of the dream we were living in the country and a creek really boarded our property. Chandelle and Marni are two of my six children, but the other children were not in the dream. Marni was younger than Chandelle.

(The two girls represent my concepts of family but that concept was coming from a feminine point of view since I only saw my female children in the dream. The creek represented emotions that the family was having to deal with.)

The water in the creek was calm, but very deep. (In real life the creek was actually shallow and no threat to the children playing around it.) The girls were playing with little turtles on the bank.

(The water, which represents emotions, was very deep and calm and didn't seem to cause a threat to the girls. They were on the shore, not quite touching the emotions yet, but were playing with turtles, which were small seemingly harmless challenges, but these challenges lived in deep water. This meant they had to do with emotions that the family was dealing with, but from my own feminine point of view, which seemed interesting but not harmful.)

My husband, Jim, and I, were watching the girls. He was concerned that the girls were playing too close to the water and told them to leave the turtles alone. I had my keys to the car with me. (We did not have house keys since our house was a small cabin that did not have a locking door.) In real life, the keys had a mace canister on them and in my dream, they also had the canister. I gave my keys to the girls and told them to take them up to the house.

(My concept of my husband was that he did not want the family involved with any emotional problems or challenges that had to do with the family, even if they seemed harmless. The keys represented the means of starting motivation. (since they belonged to the car. If they had of been house keys it would have meant they were the means of family security.) This outside motivation had to do with the family. I entrusted this motivation with the family, (giving my keys to the girls) because that was the motivation that kept me with my husband. (even at the time of the dream we were having problems with our marriage.) My security, the house was where I wanted my family to be. Secure from the world and holding the means to my outside motivation.)

My husband and I walked away, talking and ignoring the girls for awhile, thinking they had gone up to the house with the keys. After awhile I looked back at the creek and saw that the keys were floating on top, held up by the canister. I ran back to the creek, expecting the worse. I looked down in the water and could barely see the girls close to the bottom. I screamed for Jim to come because the girls had fallen into the creek.

(My husband and I had been ignoring my concept of family. (I say my concept, because my concept of family and his was different and I was seeing it from my point of view.) Because of turning our backs on the family, or girls, we had allowed our concepts to become lured by small challenges, the turtles, into deep emotions, that even though they appeared calm, were dangerous because of their depth. I came to my senses and ran to see what had happened to our family concepts and was trying to encourage Jim to pay attention to what was happening with the family because of deep emotions we were not dealing with, and did not believe were affecting the family.)

Jim did not seem concerned, but was upset that the girls had not minded us and gone up to the house, the way we asked them to do. He took his time coming to see what had happened to the girls. When he got there, I was jumping up and down, screaming for him to jump in and save the girls, since I was not a strong swimmer and he was. Still he took his time. He was dressed in his Sunday clothes and was taking off his suit coat very slowly and then his tie, and finally his shoes. I was exasperated that he was taking so long while our girls may be dead already!

(Jim's lack of concern was my concept that Jim was not as concerned for the family unit in the same way I was. His only concern seemed to be that the family was not meeting his own expectations and doing as he bid. However, I felt it was his job, not mine, to actually, save the family concept from drown in deep emotions. His clothes represented that he appeared on the outside, to me and the rest of the world, to be an upstanding, well-dressed person, but he would not shed this appearance very rapidly, even in order to save my family concepts. He was not looking within, but only concerned what we appeared to be to the rest of the world. To me, he was more concerned in his appearance as a father and a church going man, then he was concerned in what was really happening in our marriage and with our family.)

Finally, he jumped into the water. First, he brought up Marni, the youngest and the one I was closest to. She had never been very close to her father. As he brought her up, her body was limp and her long, blond hair was flowing behind her in the water. (at the time of the dream, Marni was about seven years old.) Her eyes were closed and I knew she was dead and had a terrible emotional feeling wash over me, in my dream, at the thought of her dying. When he placed her on the bank, she opened her big beautiful blue eyes, very slowly, and looked into my eyes and said, very slowly and deliberately, "I'm sorry Mother." and then she closed her eyes again and I knew she was dead. Her statement seemed to mean more than that she was just sorry that she had not minded me, but that she was sorry that she had to die, and was actually feeling sorry for me too. I woke up at that point feeling a sense of dread and fear, but knowing that the dream did not mean that my children were doing to drown.

(My concept of Jim was that he was always too late to save a situation and his lack of concern was the reason he could not help me save the family from falling apart, or drowning in emotions. He would finally try to save the family concepts but it would not be in time and the family, as I wanted it, would already be dead. Marni represented my ideal concept of family, since we were so close, and even as a baby and through her childhood, she always had to be near me to feel secure. She was beautiful and represented what I wanted a beautiful family to appear like. I felt my marriage and family life should be a s beautiful as my daughter. Her saying she was sorry, was not only my realization that it was not going to be as I had anticipated, but that there was going to be more loss than just the death of the family concepts, and Marni, in reality, would also lose her concept of father. She never became close to her father after we broke up three years later, and is still not close to her father.

The dream was a warning that if we both continued with the attitudes the way we were going, that our family concepts would die, and my own family concepts were going to die also. It would be as bad as losing one of my children, who later became "dead" to her father since they never speak, and she does not choose to get close to him.

Had I known the meaning to the dream when I dreamed it, perhaps I could have chosen to do something about it. As it turned out, I didn't change my concepts and my husband didn't change his, so we lost the family unit. Everyone suffered from it, especially my daughter Marni. It wasn't until two years after we split up, that I finally discovered what the dream had meant, but by that time, it was too late.

Overcoming inner struggles

This next dream is also a dream that I did not know the meaning of for about seven years. I also dreamed this dream while I was married and was going through a change in religious beliefs. Because it was about a black man, I thought it had to do with my concept of black people in general, but it wasn't until a black man interpreted it for me, that I really understood what it meant.

I dreamed that I was in a hexagon shaped shower stall, showering in a gym of some sort. While I was there, a black man entered the stall and started showering with me. Then he started to make love to me. I was somewhat shocked, but not really upset. My real concern was what my mother might think if she knew I was making love with a black man. (while we were racially tolerant, we were raised not to intermarry with other races, and also my mother had been raised in the south, and I knew she would disapprove of any of her children getting seriously involved with a black person.) However, I was enjoying the experience and I was torn between just letting myself enjoy what was happening, and stopping it. Finally, I stopped it and told the man that he had better go before someone came in and saw us. Even while I told him, I was feeling upset at his leaving, but my concerns for what my mother and others might thing was stronger than my need of his attention. We walked out to the dressing room together, holding hands. Even as I wanted him to go, I had the feeling that he was important to me and he had an important message or lesson to teach me. A large crowd of people started to come in, so I encouraged him to leave before they could see us. However, they got where we were before he could leave and I was surprised that no one said anything or even seemed to notice that we were together and that we had no clothes on. Then I felt good about him being there, but I saw that he had gotten lost in the crowd and we became separated. I felt a great sense of loss and tried to follow him, but couldn't get to him. I woke up with the impression of his face in my mind and could not forget the dream until I discovered what it meant.

Meaning

The shower represented soft cleansing emotions that I was engulfed in at the time. (my search for a more fulfilling spiritual belief) The shape of the stall indicated that there were many sides involved in this search that surrounded me. The black man was a new concept that entered the stall and embraced me. He was seen as black because the spiritual concepts that I was starting to embrace, would not be approved of by my mother, any more than she would approve of me having a close personal relationship with a black man. It would appear as a black concept to her, and so in my dream, I saw it as a black concept also. However, I was feeling fulfilled by this concept, as my spiritual knowledge in that direction was becoming stronger and more fulfilling in real life. I also worried more about what my mother would think of me, changing my beliefs, and felt I should not get involved, no matter how right it felt.

My concerns of what the rest of the world would think, if they found me with a black man, was my concerns of what others would think of my concepts that I was starting to embrace as a new belief. On one hand, I wanted to stay with the black man because I thought he had something of importance to impart to me, (my need to gain something from this new spiritual concept) but on the other hand, I didn't want to be seen nude with him. (my fear of allowing my true self-expression to be seen by others) When the crowd came, I discovered that no one noticed anyway,. The indication that my beliefs were not going to be scrutinized by the outside world. My sense of loss was that I had doubted my own instincts and allowed outside influences to sway me in my own beliefs. The deep impression of his face was the tool that kept me questioning the dream until I actually discovered the meaning, after seeing a photo of a black man who looked like the man in my dream. Later, when we became friends, he gave his insight on the dream.

These are just a few examples of dreams and explanations to their meanings. Now it is your turn. It is not real important to go over every little detail of your dream to discover the meaning of each symbol. After a while the dream will be seen as an overall picture, rather than a lot of little symbols to be dealt with. Mostly you should be concerned with those symbols that have impressed you the most in your dream. Try to get the overall feel of what your entire dream was dealing with and then look at the symbols as filling in the gaps. Writing the dream down will help you discover how the dream influences you, or eventually comes to pass. You can discover if it warned you of some future event, and then you will have a better handle on understanding when you have those kind of dreams and can avoid changes in your life you do not want to experience, or you need to deal with, instead of ignore.

If you don't have time to write your dreams down, at least go over each dream that you have, in your mind, at awakening, before you get out of bed, or start doing daily activities. Go over each piece of your dream as you can remember it, to get it solid in your mind. Even if you end up forgetting it during the day, going over it in your mind, helps to transfer the dream from the inner self to the outer self and it will have its influences on you more readily that way.

If you have any future questions about dreams or dreaming, feel free to write me at <u>Wahconda@hotmail.com</u>. I may not know all the answers to what you may ask, but exchanging information is the best way of discovering new ideas and gaining new knowledge. Make the subject to your letters, "Questions about analyzing dreams" so I will know it is not junk mail..

I hope all your dreams are pleasant ones.

Jeanie